Think Outside The Box

Leading Diversity & Inclusion
in the Workplace

John Duncan, 2019

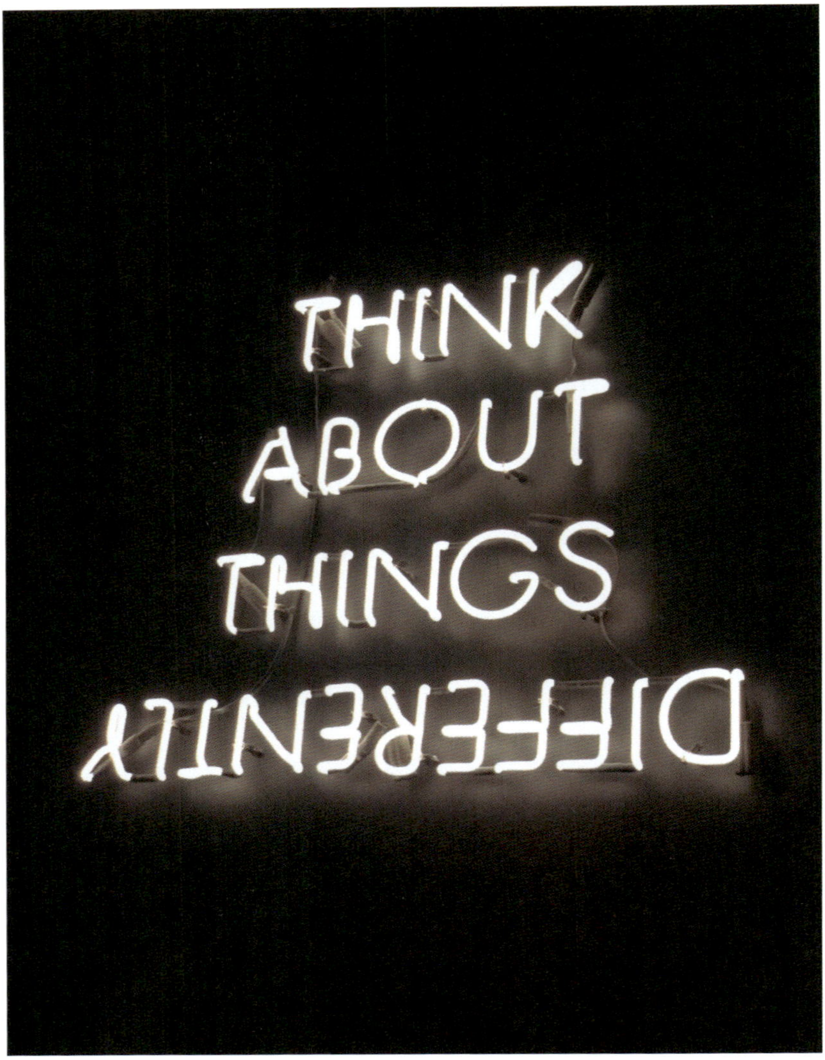
THINK
ABOUT
THINGS
DIFFERENTLY

"Diversity is being invited to the party; inclusion is being asked to dance"

Verna Myers, Diversity & Inclusion Activist,
Vice President, Inclusion Strategy at Netflix

Contents

Description	Page

Part 1 – The Equality Act 2010 – Legislation in the Workplace

- The Business Case for Diversity • 11
- Defining Diversity and Inclusion • 13
- The Equality Act 2010 – An Introduction • 17
- The Equality Act 2010 - Protected Characteristics • 19
- Discrimination in the workplace • 21
- Stereotypes • 23
- Workplace Bias • 25
- Workplace Bullying and Harassment • 27
- The Human Rights Act • 29
- The Public Sector Equality Duty • 31
- The Gender Pay Gap • 33

Part 2 – Leading Diversity and Inclusion in an Organisation

- Political Correctness or a Tick-Box Exercise? • 38
- Workplace Inequalities • 40
- Who Leads D&I in an Organisation? • 42
- Asking Questions of your D&I Practices • 44
- Example Diversity & Inclusion Action Plan • 45
- Implementing Diversity & Inclusion Good Practice • 46
- Managing Change and Continuous Improvement • 48
- Equality Impact Assessments • 50
- Workplace Diversity & Inclusion Training • 52
- Make an Impact - Getting Things Done • 54
- The 1st 100 Days - Policy, Strategy & Quick Wins • 56
- Reporting Impact of D&I Measures to Leaders • 58
- National Centre for Diversity, Stonewall and Inclusive Employers • 60

Description	Page

Part 3 – Workplace Strategies to Improve Diversity and Inclusion

- Hints, Tips & Other Strategies to Build Inclusion   • 62
- Advancing Equality for Disabled Staff   • 64
- Ramadan Mubarak – How to Support Employees Observing Ramadan   • 66
- Flexible Working for New Dads   • 68
- Improving LBGT Inclusion in the Workplace   • 70
- Positive Action for Under Representation   • 72
- Staff Networks   • 74
- Know the Diversity & Inclusion Calendar   • 76

Part 4 – Case Studies – Inequality in Action

- Case Study 1 – Community Tensions   • 78
- Case Study 2 – Racial Discrimination   • 79
- Case Study 3 – Gender Discrimination   • 81
- Case Study 4 – Under Represented Groups   • 82
- Case Study 5 – Exclusion   • 84

Summary – Culture First, Diversity and Inclusion Second   • 87

Diversity & Inclusion – A Glossary of Terms   • 91

References   • 94

Introduction

Diversity and Inclusion recognises that historically certain groups of people with protected characteristics such as race, disability, sex and sexual orientation have experienced discrimination. Whereas, equality is about ensuring that every individual has an equal opportunity to make the most of their lives and talents. As such, equality, diversity and inclusion attempts to ensure that no one should have poorer life chances because of their gender, their race, the way they were born, where they come from, what they believe, who they love, or whether they have a disability.

Subsequently, Equality, Diversity and Inclusion becomes less about compliance with legislation and more about leading change, improvement initiatives, engaging, motivating and improving the potential of staff.

Diversity and Inclusion - let's refer to it as D&I from now on - can sometimes be seen - quite inaccurately - as a minefield of political correctness or an exercise in 'box ticking' in order to satisfy government legislation. Nevertheless, in recent years, organisations have become increasingly aware of the business case for being an inclusive organisation, one where employees feel valued, opportunities are available for all and diversity is celebrated. That said, it is worth noting that the British workplace has experienced diversity and inclusion initiatives in many different ways over the past twenty years, usually involving phrases such as 'equal opportunities', 'equality, diversity & inclusion' and much more recently the simplification 'diversity & inclusion'.

In general, accountability for D&I initiatives in a large organisation were added to the responsibilities of an existing role, usually to a senior leader or the human resources department and often seen as a burden or at best an administrative inconvenience. However, over the past few years, we have seen a clear shift in business culture around diversity; in particular larger organisations who are beginning to take D&I more seriously. This is clearly demonstrated by the sharp rise in a range of very specific job roles now being advertised, including roles such as Head of Equality, Diversity & Inclusion, EDI Workforce Lead, D&I Manager and E&D Coordinator. Subsequently, this book is for those leaders new to such a role, or anyone who holds responsibility for diversity and inclusion in their workplace.

There are very few 'how to' guides for leaders of D&I with practical methods to actually lead improvements, overcome challenges and measure impact and improvement. Whilst there is a wide range of academic literature available on the subject, they tend to be almost exclusively based in academic theory rather than practice. As such, 'Think Outside The Box - Leading Diversity & Inclusion in the Workplace' is designed to tackle this problem by providing workplace D&I leaders with practical, real world strategies that enable them to engage with staff in ways which are both meaningful and impactful, serving as a contemporary and up-to-date source of D&I best practice.

The author - John Duncan - is a diversity and inclusion specialist leading on strategy and policy development with over 15 years substantial experience of providing advice, support and training within the public sector. You can read more about workplace diversity and inclusion via his regular blog at theequalityblog.co.uk.

"Here are the values that I stand for: honesty, equality, kindness, compassion, treating people the way you want to be treated and helping those in need. To me, those are traditional values."

Ellen DeGeneres, comedian.

The Business Case for Diversity

Increasingly, the term 'Equality' (and what used to be referred to as Equal Opportunities) is making way for discussions on 'diversity' as this term is much broader in its scope and gets to the heart of the integration challenges facing the UK workforce.

Over the past five decades Britain has become increasingly complex and multicultural as population growth continues, subsequently becoming more diverse and with an aging population. Furthermore, changes to employment law coupled with automation and a rise in the retirement age means we now have increased competition in the workplace for fewer and fewer jobs.

As Vijay Eswaran, Executive Chairman, QI Group of Companies, explains: 'In this era of globalization, diversity in the business environment is about more than gender, race and ethnicity. It now includes employees with diverse religious and political beliefs, education, socioeconomic backgrounds, sexual orientation, cultures and even disabilities. Companies are discovering that, by supporting and promoting a diverse and inclusive workplace, they are gaining benefits that go beyond the optics.'[1]

In the UK, it's common for staff, when surveyed in the workplace, to perceive diversity as being a focus on ethnicity and race whereas issues of religion, education or culture are often overlooked or misunderstood. Subsequently, diversity is actually a much broader term than a few labels and includes those other – difficult to define - human qualities that are dissimilar to our own perceptions or those of our communities but are widely prevalent in other communities. It's this fundamental difference that diversity looks to both celebrate and include alongside our own perceptions.

Vijay Eswaran argues that workplace diversity leads to greater innovation. 'The coming together of people of different ethnicities with different experiences in cities and societies is a key driver of innovation. The food that we eat every day is a result of this blending of cultures. The most successful musical genres, such as jazz, rock'n'roll or hip-hop, are the products of cultural amalgamation.'

Whilst recent equality laws have helped to challenge discrimination and prejudice, we still face equality gaps in the workplace, some larger than others. In response to the increasingly diverse needs of our communities the government have delegated a duty of responsibility – known as the Public Sector Equality Duty - on councils and their partners, including publicly funded bodes, such as the education and health care sectors, to be more accountable for ensuring everyone has an equal chance in life regardless of background or start in life.

To this end, in order to meet both government legislation as well as the diverse needs of our workforce, organisations must ensure they build an inclusive culture where diversity and equality of opportunity work hand in hand. This is referred to as the business case for diversity, an organisational wide understanding of how diversity can benefit both the business aims of the organisation and the needs of the community.

Defining Diversity & Inclusion

Diversity and Inclusion has seen a range of terms which describe similar attempts to make improvements for those with protected characteristics. First we had Equal Opportunities, and then came Equality & Diversity (E&D), this was then expanded to Equality, Diversity & Inclusion (EDI) and in more recent times this has been simplified to Diversity & Inclusion (D&I). In truth, the quiet removal, in recent years, of the term equality from equality, diversity & inclusion was because equality suggests that everyone is at a particular starting point and should be treated the same. It seeks to promote fairness, but it can only work if everyone starts from the same place and needs the same level of support. As such, diversity and inclusion are more focused on redressing historical discrimination and can have a much greater impact.

However, equality is still important and refers to a state of being equal; in law equality refers to being equal in relation to an individual's status, rights or opportunity. As such, in relation to the workforce, 'equality' is synonymous with terms such as fairness, equal opportunities, impartiality, even-handedness, egalitarianism, equal rights, non-discrimination, even justice, freedom and emancipation are linked to equality. The Trade Union Congress

13

(TUC) define equality as *'ensuring everybody has an equal opportunity, and is not treated differently or discriminated against because of their characteristics.'*[2]

In broader terms, equality sets out to build a fairer society where everyone is able to participate and people have the opportunity to reach their full potential. Importantly, equality is supported in law and legislation is designed to tackle prejudice and discrimination. However, equality in the work place suffers from some misconceptions and it's important to dispel these misunderstandings that equality is not about tokenism, it is not about doing people favours, and it's not about lowering of standards, nor is it a numbers game.

As such, with regard to the workforce, equality is about guaranteeing staff have equal opportunity for participation, development and promotion whilst not being discriminated against because of their differences. In fact, as Frances O'Grady explains it, in her book 2012 book, Breaking Through The Barriers – *'Regardless of age, race, gender, class, sexual orientation, religion or belief, disability or the passport they hold, every worker should enjoy an equal chance to up-skill or learn something new at work.'*[3]

Despite legislation and wide ranging professional support for equality in the workplace there are still all too familiar examples where equality is not happening. Across industry sectors we still see workplace situations where women earn less than men. Furthermore, black and minority ethnic groups are still achieving below their white British peers in terms of education and are underrepresented in the jobs they do when compared to people from other groups. Also, part-time staff, including temporary and shift workers, may not always have access to training or opportunities to progress at work which their full time colleagues benefit from.

Whilst equality is about opportunity diversity is about recognising and valuing difference in our society. What diversity asks of us is so important because it asks us to create a culture and working practices that recognise, respect, value and harness differences for the benefit of the organisation and individual.

According to the Institute of Leadership and Management, diversity can be defined as: 'The variety of experiences and perspective which arise from differences in race, culture, religion, mental or physical abilities, heritage, age, gender, sexual orientation, gender identity and other characteristics.'[4]

As Patel and Yafai explain in their book Demystifying Diversity 'Today there is far more movement both within a country and across borders than ever before in human history. In London alone there are over 300 languages spoken in schools with more than 100 different languages spoken in virtually every London Borough.'[5]

However, diversity does not stop at recognising and valuing the difference between people from different cultures it also looks to accept that people from different backgrounds may operate in a different, even alien, way than we are not used to. To this end, diversity seeks to ensure that those differences are allowed for and actually add value to the culture and working practices of an organisation.

When assessing now well your organisation values diversity it is important to consider the workplace experiences of people who may be different, due to their:

- Gender
- Religion
- Ethnic Origin
- Marital Status
- Nationality
- Sexual Orientation
- Culture
- Age

Differences like these have historically led to some situations where an individual or a group/cohort may be treated unfairly. As such, if a person feels they are being discriminated against or treated unfairly due to one of these differences then they are protected in law by the Equality Act 2010 and could, in some situations, turn to an employment tribunal or other legal method of challenging this.

However, it is important to remember that the legal route is not the only consequence of unfair treatment or discrimination because it will also lead to low morale in the affected groups, potential strike action, disputes between staff and the skills and abilities of those affected may be poorly utilised by the organisation.

Though, as Nerlarine Cornelius reminds us in the book Building Workplace Equality, '…whether you label the efforts as equal opportunities or diversity is not critical to effective intervention in this area, so long as the essence is owned and understood by those people who are likely to be affected by it.'[6] The key here is communication and ensuring that those most affected by diversity initiatives have some say in them.

The Equality Act 2010 – An Introduction

The Equality Act 2010 came into force on 1st October 2010 and was introduced to bring together a complex set of overlapping legislation into one simplified and harmonious Act. This new Act brought together previous legislation including the Equal Pay Act 1970, the Sex Discrimination Act 1975, the Race Relations Act 1976, the Disability Discrimination Act 1995 and additional delegated legislation which prevented discrimination in employment on the basis of religion, belief, sexual orientation and age.

Whilst in general the Act covers employment and strengthens laws to give greater protection to employees from discrimination it does also cover some aspects of discrimination outside of employment. Most significantly, the Equality Act 2010 sets out a requirement for employers to assure equal treatment in access to employment as well as private and public services, regardless of the individuals 'protected characteristics', which are listed below.

- Age
- Disability
- Gender Reassignment
- Marriage and Civil Partnership
- Pregnancy and Maternity
- Race
- Religion or Belief
- Sex
- Sexual orientation

These 'protected characteristics' represent a defining guide to safeguard employees from unfair treatment or discrimination but in the case of disability, employers and service providers are under a duty to make reasonable adjustments to their workplaces to overcome barriers experienced by disabled people.

Through the Equality Act 2010 employees are explicitly protected from discrimination by any of these protected characteristics and so employers must be mindful of how their procedures, policies and practices impact on their employees and where necessary review accordingly.

In order for an organisation to ensure it is meeting the requirements of the Act it is highly recommended, but not legally required, that an equality & diversity policy is in place, especially for larger organisations. In fact, for larger organisations, the publishing of an equality & diversity policy on the company website will demonstrate that the organisation is committed to meeting its legal and ethical obligations towards being an inclusive employer. Furthermore, by having the policy in place and publically available it can contribute towards making its employees more comfortable at the organisation and encourage everyone in the organisation to treat others equally.

The Equality Act 2010 - Protected Characteristics

Through the 'Protected Characteristics' the Equality Act 2010 ensures that it is unlawful to discriminate against someone because of any of these characteristics which are defined by the University of Sheffield[7] as:

1. **Age** - The Act protects people of all ages. However, different treatment because of age is not unlawful direct or indirect discrimination if you can justify it (for example if you can demonstrate that it is a proportionate means of meeting a legitimate aim). Age is the only protected characteristic that allows employers to justify direct discrimination.

2. **Disability** - The Act has made it easier for a person to show that they are disabled and protected from disability discrimination. Under the Act, a person is disabled if they have a physical or mental impairment which has a substantial and long term adverse effect on their ability to carry out normal day-to-day activities, which would include things like using a telephone, reading a book or using public transport.

3. **Gender reassignment -** The Act provides protection for transsexual people. A transsexual person is someone who proposes to, starts or has completed a process to change his or her gender. The Act no longer requires a person to be under medical supervision to be protected – so a woman who decides to live as a man but does not undergo any medical procedures would be covered.

4. **Marriage and civil partnership -** The Act protects employees who are married or in a civil partnership against discrimination. Single people are not protected.

5. **Pregnancy and maternity -** A woman is protected against discrimination on the grounds of pregnancy and maternity during the period of her pregnancy and any statutory maternity leave to which she is entitled. During this period, pregnancy and maternity discrimination cannot be treated as sex discrimination. You must not take into account an employee´s period of absence due to pregnancy-related illness when making a decision about her employment.

6. **Race -** For the purposes of the Act `race´ includes colour, nationality and ethnic or national origins.

7. **Religion or belief -** In the Equality Act, religion includes any religion. It also includes no religion, in other words employees or jobseekers are protected if they do not follow a certain religion or have no religion at all. Additionally, a religion must have a clear structure and belief system.

8. **Sex -** Both men and women are protected under the Act.

9. **Sexual orientation -** The Act protects bisexual, gay, heterosexual and lesbian people.

Discrimination in the Workplace

Discrimination is where an individual or group of individuals are treated differently due to their perceived membership of a certain group or social category. For example, an individual or group of individuals may suffer discrimination because they are from the Travelling Community. Under the Equality Act 2010 it is unlawful to discriminate against any individual (or group) based upon any of the protected characteristics. In the workplace, this can take many forms including black workers not being offered the same opportunity as white workers, women being paid less than men for doing the same job but can include age, colour, convictions, height, disability, ethnicity, family status, gender identity, genetic characteristics, marital status, nationality, race, religion, sex or sexual orientation.

Direct Discrimination

Direct discrimination is where an individual is treated differently or worse than others for certain reasons, it is often easy to spot such as being refused entry to a hotel because you are gay. The Citizens Advice Bureau describes direct discrimination through the following example: *'You're a saleswoman and you inform your employer that you want to spend the rest of your life living as a man. As a result of this, you're moved to a role without client contact against your wishes. This is less favourable treatment because of gender reassignment. It would still be less favourable treatment even if your employer were to increase your salary to make up for the loss of job status.'*[8]

Indirect Discrimination

There are other times when you appear to be treated equally and in the same way as others but it actually has a worse impact on you because of who you are. This is known as indirect discrimination where a workplace practice, policy or rule applies to all but it has a worse effect on some than others. The Citizens Advice Bureau describes indirect discrimination through the following example: *'A health club only accepts customers who are on the electoral register. This applies to all customers in the same way. But Gypsies and Travellers are less likely to be on the electoral register and therefore they'll find it more difficult to join. This could be indirect discrimination against Gypsies and Travellers because of the protected characteristic of race. The rule seems fair, but it has a worse effect on this particular group of people.'*[8]

Justifying Discrimination

Not all discrimination is unlawful, if an employer treats you unfairly because of who you are they might have a good enough reason but may have to justify their discrimination. The Citizens Advice Bureau describes justifying discrimination through the following example: *'A hospital advertises a surgeon's job for which it requires at least ten years' experience. You can't meet this requirement because you've taken time off work to care for your children. As you're a woman, this looks like indirect discrimination because of sex. But the hospital may be able to justify this, if it can show that the job can't be done properly without that amount of experience. This is likely to be a legitimate aim.'[8]*

Stereotypes

Regrettably, stereotyping still occurs in our workplaces and is, in general, because of outdated and inaccurate views of certain groups in society. A stereotype can be said to be a commonly held but oversimplified image or idea of a particular type of person or social group.

Some stereotypes are regarding a different culture such as the concept of the Frenchman wearing a black beret with a string of onions around his neck. Some stereotypes are about individuals or social groups such the stereotype that woman are carers, or men are strong and do all the work, or all Arabs and Muslims are terrorists, Irish people are drunks and eat potatoes, or that any feminine man is gay and any masculine woman is a lesbian. Stereotypes can sometimes be misinterpreted by others as just prejudice because they too are based upon a prior assumption about people from different cultures and races. However, where prejudice is a deliberate act stereotyping can come from ignorance of the facts or a lack of education around the subject.

Most cultures have some form of negative stereotype associated with them including black people, the Irish, those from the Middle East, the Polish, the Travelling community and Jewish people. However, gender stereotyping occurs where, for example, if you say that all women like to cook, you are stereotyping women. Similarly, stereotypes regarding a person's sexual orientation are common and these stereotypes occur when someone has negative views on gays, lesbians, and transgender individuals.

Combatting Negative Stereotypes in the Workplace

Stereotyping can lead people to hide some aspects of their lives from society, for example members of the gay or lesbian community may be afraid to admit their sexuality for fear of being judged. This can lead to the victims of stereotyping to have their lives led by fear.

As such, stereotypes have no place in the modern workplace and it is important that an organisation is seen as inclusive where a woman can work in construction, a man can work as a nurse, a man can work part-time, or be a carer and a wheelchair is no barrier to opportunity. A strong message from senior leaders is needed to demonstrate this vision and reinforce that negative stereotyping will not be tolerated.

Training can help where negative stereotypes are prevalent and certain industry sectors are more likely to attract a workforce with negative stereotypes than others. However, it is wrong to assume a more educated workforce means a more inclusive one; the well-educated can be as equally likely to hold some negative stereotypes of others as low skilled or poorly educated members of the workforce.

To this end, if you need to identify where negative stereotypes are prevalent in your organisation then a staff survey can help point you in the right direction. Certainly, it will help you identify, albeit anonymously, areas of the organisation who feel they are victims of stereotyping which is a start in being able to educate a workforce and remove negative and damaging stereotypes from the workplace.

Workplace Bias

Generally speaking, bias is a preference or prejudice for or against one person or group, especially in a way considered to be unfair. For example, an employer may give preferential treatment to potential employees from the same socioeconomic background as themselves. Alternatively, a manager my show bias through only offering development opportunities to female members of staff.

According to Robert Booth and Aamna Mohdin[10], writing for the Guardian newspaper in 2018, the extent to which ethnic minorities still suffer from bias is quite staggering. They commissioned a survey for the Guardian newspaper of 1,000 people from minority ethnic backgrounds who found they were consistently more likely to have faced negative everyday experiences – all frequently associated with racism – than white people in a comparison poll.

The survey found that 43% of those from a minority ethnic background had been overlooked for a work promotion in a way that felt unfair in the last five years – more than twice the proportion of white people (18%) who reported the same experience. Furthermore, the results show that ethnic minorities are three times as likely to have been thrown out of or denied entrance to a restaurant, bar or

25

club in the last five years, and that more than two-thirds believe Britain has a problem with racism.

The article went on to explain the Runnymede Trust, a racial equality think tank, described the findings as "stark" and said they illustrated "everyday micro-aggressions" that had profound effects on Britain's social structure. What's more, the survey revealed that Muslims living in Britain – a large minority at around 2.8 million people – are more likely to have negative experiences than other religious groups. They are more likely than Christians, people with no religion and other smaller religions to be stopped by the police, left out of social functions at work or college and find that people seem not to want to sit next to them on public transport.

The effects of bias are not the same for all ethnicities. Half of black and mixed-race people felt they had been unfairly overlooked for a promotion or job application, compared with 41% of people from Asian backgrounds. Black people were more likely to feel they had to work harder to succeed because of their ethnicity.

It also found troubling levels of concern about bias in the workplace, with 57% of minorities saying they felt they had to work harder to succeed in Britain because of their ethnicity, and 40% saying they earned less or had worse employment prospects for the same reason.

Workplace bias needs to be combated through education and a change in attitudes across an organisation. Where a culture of inclusion exists in an organisation you will find bias is greatly reduced and staff survey results will indicate a better level of satisfaction from groups open to historical workplace bias.

Workplace Bullying and Harassment

Whilst bullying and harassment in the workplace is clearly something no organisation wants to see happening in their own back yard the law can actually confuse the matter further because bullying in the workplace is not actually unlawful but harassment is. However, employers are expected to have a zero tolerance towards bullying and harassment and to take action when it has been identified to protect working relationships.

Bullying and harassment can take different forms, some highly aggressive and obvious whilst others can be more subtle and less obvious. Bullying is rarely isolated and is often a pattern of behaviour where a number of incidents demonstrate that it is taking place. According to ACAS[11], the Advisory, Conciliation and Arbitration Service, bullying and harassment in the workplace may include:

- spreading malicious rumours, or insulting someone by word or behaviour (particularly on the grounds of age, race, sex, disability, sexual orientation and religion or belief)
- copying memos that are critical about someone to others who do not need to know
- ridiculing or demeaning someone - picking on them or setting them up to fail
- exclusion or victimisation
- unfair treatment
- overbearing supervision or other misuse of power or position
- unwelcome sexual advances - touching, standing too close, the display of offensive materials, asking for sexual favours, making decisions on the basis of sexual advances being accepted or rejected
- making threats or comments about job security without foundation
- deliberately undermining a competent worker by overloading and constant criticism
- preventing individuals progressing by intentionally blocking promotion or training opportunities.

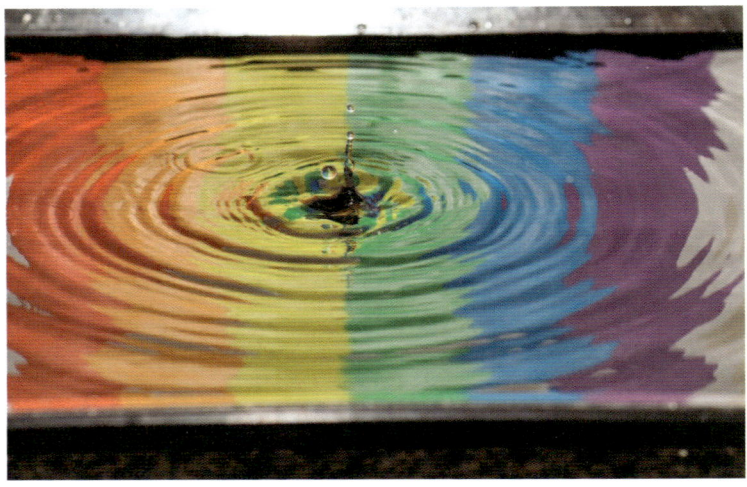

Harassment should not be tolerated in the workplace and under the Equality Act 2010 it is unlawful and whilst an employer has a duty to implement the act it is not required in law to have a policy regarding bullying and harassment. That said, it is certainly good practice to do so and most human resources departments will have one in place in order to be very clear on what is and what is not acceptable so workplace bullies can be held to account.

It is often useful for a D&I lead to examine the records of bullying and harassment claims/allegations in an organisation to see if there is a wider issue that requires intervention, training or policy changes in order to reduced such incidents.

The Human Rights Act

In the UK, the fundamental rights and freedoms of its population are set out in the Human Rights Act 1998 and incorporates those rights as set out in the European Convention on Human Rights (ECHR) and ensures they are covered in domestic British law.

According to the Equality and Human Rights Commission[12], *'the Act sets out our human rights in a series of 'Articles'. Each Article deals with a different right. These are all taken from the ECHR and are commonly known as 'the Convention Rights':*

- Article 2: Right to life
- Article 3: Freedom from torture and inhuman or degrading treatment
- Article 4: Freedom from slavery and forced labour
- Article 5: Right to liberty and security
- Article 6: Right to a fair trial
- Article 7: No punishment without law
- Article 8: Respect for your private and family life, home and correspondence
- Article 9: Freedom of thought, belief and religion
- Article 10: Freedom of expression
- Article 11: Freedom of assembly and association
- Article 12: Right to marry and start a family
- Article 14: Protection from discrimination in respect of these rights and freedoms
- Protocol 1, Article 1: Right to peaceful enjoyment of your property
- Protocol 1, Article 2: Right to education
- Protocol 1, Article 3: Right to participate in free elections
- Protocol 13, Article 1: Abolition of the death penalty

The Equality and Human Rights Commission identify three main effects of the Act:

1. You can seek justice in a British court - It incorporates the rights set out in the European Convention on Human Rights (ECHR) into domestic British law. This means that if your human rights have been breached, you can take your case to a British court rather than having to seek justice from the European Court of Human Rights in Strasbourg, France.

2. Public bodies must respect your rights - It requires all public bodies (like courts, police, local authorities, hospitals and publicly funded schools) and other bodies carrying out public functions to respect and protect your human rights.

3. New laws are compatible with Convention rights - In practice it means that Parliament will nearly always make sure that new laws are compatible with the rights set out in the European Convention on Human Rights (although ultimately Parliament is sovereign and can pass laws which are incompatible). The courts will also, where possible, interpret laws in a way which is compatible with Convention rights.

Public Sector Equality Duty

Equality, Diversity and Inclusion is not just about compliance with legislation, it's about leading change, improvement initiatives, engaging, motivating and improving the potential of staff. The Public Sector Equality Duty (PSED) brings this into law for all public bodies in the United Kingdom.

According to ACAS[13] (the Advisory, Conciliation and Arbitration Service) the Public Sector Equality Duty requires public bodies and others carrying out public functions to have due regard to the need to eliminate discrimination, to advance equality of opportunities and foster good relations. The duty applies to all nine areas of discrimination listed in the Equality Act 2010.

As such, it's about ensuring all stakeholders are at the centre of the services offered to the public and positively impacting upon the context and culture of the organisation whilst supporting public sector staff to design and deliver great service.

The role of the Public Sector Equality Duty is to eliminate unlawful discrimination, harassment, victimisation and any other conduct prohibited by the Equality Act 2010. To advance equality of opportunity between people who share a protected characteristic and people who do not share it foster good relations between people who share a protected characteristic and those who do not.

It is a requirement in law that public bodies such as the NHS, local government, police, fire brigades, schools, colleges, universities and others carrying out public functions follow the Public Sector Equality Duty. The full list of employers required to follow the PSED can be found in Schedule 19 of the Equality Act 2010.

The duty applies to individual employees, workers, contractors and customer and all nine areas of discrimination listed in the Equality Act 2010 – referred to as protected characteristics - meaning that employers need to consider:

- age
- disability
- gender reassignment
- pregnancy and maternity
- race
- religion or belief
- sex
- sexual orientation
- marriage and civil partnership

Note: For marriage and civil partnership, the Public Sector Equality Duty only requires employers to have due regard to the need to eliminate unlawful discrimination.

This ensures that public bodies consider the needs of all individuals in their day to day work - in shaping policy, in delivering services, and in relation to their own employees.

The Gender Pay Gap

Diversity and inclusion initiatives are designed to redress the balance where decades of inequality have led to high levels of disparity in the workplace. Gender Pay Gap reporting is no different and the Equality Act 2010 makes it a statutory duty for organisations with more than 250 employees to report on their gender pay gap, which looks to redress the long standing percentage difference between average hourly earnings for men and women. Currently, the national average mean gender pay gap is 17.9%, which indicates - on average - woman in the UK earn 17.9% less than men. In fact, the Guardian[14] (April 2019) reported that a quarter of companies and public sector bodies have a pay gap of more than 20% in favour of men. However, according to the Financial Times[15] (23 April 2019), Government policymakers hoped the transparency would shame large employers into taking swift action to narrow the difference between what they pay men and women.

What is the Gender Pay Gap?

The gender pay gap shows the difference between the average (mean or median) earnings of men and women. This is expressed as a percentage of men's earnings e.g. women earn 15% less than men. Used to its full potential, gender pay gap reporting is a valuable tool for assessing levels of equality in the workplace, female and male participation, and how effectively talent is being maximised.

What is the difference between the gender pay gap and equal pay?

It's worth noting that a gender pay gap isn't the same as unequal pay. Equal pay - where men and women doing the same job should be paid the same - has been a legal requirement for nearly fifty years. Under the Equal Pay Act 1970, and more recently, the Equality Act 2010, it is unlawful to pay people unequally because they are a man or a woman. This applies to all employers, no matter how small. As such, a company might have a gender pay gap if a majority of men are in top jobs, despite paying male and female employees the same amount for similar roles.

The gender pay gap shows the differences in the average pay between men and women. If a workplace has a particularly high gender pay gap, this can indicate there may be a number of issues to deal with, and the individual calculations may help to identify what those issues are. In some cases, the gender pay gap may include unlawful inequality in pay but this is not necessarily the case.

What is the Median pay gap?

The median pay gap is the difference in pay between the middle-ranking woman and the middle-ranking man.

If you place all the men and women working at a company into two lines in order of salary, the median pay gap will be the difference in salary between the woman in the middle of her line and the man in the middle of his.

What is the Mean pay gap?

The mean pay gap is the difference between a company's total wage spend-per-woman and its total spend-per-man.

The number is calculated by taking the total wage bill for each and dividing it by the number of men and women employed by the organisation.

Why is there a Gender Pay Gap?

According to the BBC[16], there's no one reason behind the gender pay gap - it's a complex issue.

The Fawcett Society[17], a group which campaigns for equality, says caring responsibilities can play a big part. Women often care for young children or elderly relatives. This means women are more likely to work in part-time roles, which are often lower paid or have fewer opportunities for progression. Another important factor is a divided labour market. Women are still more likely to work in lower-paid and lower-skilled jobs. Women currently make up 62% of those earning less than the living wage, according to the Living Wage Foundation. Discrimination is another cause of the gender pay gap.

The Equality and Human Rights Commission[18] (ECHR) has previously found that one in nine new mothers were either dismissed, made redundant or treated so poorly they felt they had to leave their job. This can create a gap in experience, leading to lower wages when women return to work.

Men also tend to take up the majority of the most senior roles at a company, which are the highest paid.

Who has to publish Gender Pay Gap data?

As stated earlier, it is a legal requirement for all employers (with 250 or more employees) to publish their gender pay report within one year of the 'snapshot' date, which is usually the end of March. However, whilst all employers must comply with the reporting regulations - for employers whose headcount varies they must comply with the reporting regulations for any year where they had a headcount of 250 or more employees on the 'snapshot' date.

What information needs to be published?

The following information must be reported by organisations:

- Their mean gender pay gap
- Their median gender pay gap
- Their mean bonus gender pay gap
- Their median bonus gender pay gap
- Their proportion of males receiving a bonus payment
- Their proportion of females receiving a bonus payment
- Their proportion of males and females in each quartile pay band
- A written statement, authorised by an appropriate senior person, which confirms the accuracy of their calculations. However, this requirement only applies to employers subject to the Equality Act 2010 (Gender Pay Gap Information) Regulations 2017.

Can companies be punished for a wide gender pay gap?

According to Lorna Jones[16], Business Reporter, BBC News, companies can't be punished for a wide gender pay gap. But they might be punished for failing to publish their data, or for publishing inaccurate or misleading figures.

The Equality and Human Rights Commission[18] (EHRC) is responsible for ensuring employers publish their pay gap figures. The EHRC set out plans for its enforcement policy in December. The EHRC says it will approach employers informally at first, but businesses could ultimately face "unlimited fines and convictions".

As the EHRC is still consulting on these plans, it remains to be seen whether they can or will punish companies in this way. At the moment, there is no enforcement mechanism in the regulations on publishing pay gap data. The UK government says it will also publish sector-specific league tables, highlighting companies failing to address pay differences between men and women.

What can organisations do to reduce the Gender Pay Gap?

According to Dharishini David[19], Economics Correspondent with the BBC, gender pay gap reporting may not be enough: the government may need to get tougher. Ask gender pay specialists how to solve the problem and they'll tell you there are many initiatives that companies can take - tackling unconscious bias, offering more flexible working and encouraging shared parental leave.

However, the issue doesn't end at the office door. The experts say society needs to change. For example, schools could encourage girls to take more STEM subjects: science, technology, engineering and maths. There should be more flexible, affordable childcare options. And men could take on more of the household chores.

On the other hand, societal change takes time, sometimes a generation, and currently we can report on the organisations gender pay gaps and look for short term internal solutions but overall society needs to change its attitude to gender, specifically in relation to employment, if we are to have pay equality across gender.

Political Correctness or a Tick-Box Exercise?

When leading D&I in an organisation it is not unusual to face challenges and barriers to achieving your targets from a common misconception as to what equality and diversity is all about. First and foremost, equality, diversity and inclusion is about people and not a 'tick box' exercise to satisfy government/employer statistics or legislation.

Perhaps the most common misconception reported by equality and diversity trainers is that D&I is often said - behind closed doors of course - to be 'just political correctness' or sometimes 'political correctness gone mad'. Political correctness can be defined as *'the avoidance of forms of expression or action that are perceived to exclude, marginalize, or insult groups of people who are socially disadvantaged or discriminated against'.* It is often the term 'forms of expression' from definitions such as this which some interpret to mean jokes or work place banter. However, where someone is offended by your words it is not open to your interpretation it is open to theirs, as such if your opinion, jokes or workplace banter offends people then it is time keep such options, jokes or work place banter out of the workplace. To those who question whether equality and diversity is merely 'political correctness gone mad' I would ask the question whether it is acceptable for woman to be paid less than men for the same job, for part time staff or shift workers to have less opportunities in training, for the LGBTQ+ community to face harassment at work or for those from a minority to be excluded from jobs because of a different place of birth? Sometimes, D&I needs to focus the minds of those not affected to understand how a lack of D&I impacts those with protected characteristics and how they can help combat this and bring fairness to their workplace.

However, even when supported, D&I can still be viewed by some in the workplace as a 'box to tick' exercise or just another thing on a long list of other things that they are required to do by government. This fundamental lack of understanding as to the need for D&I practices often leads to a misunderstanding of intended actions and their outcomes which in its self often leads to a compartmentalised, tick-box approach. Nevertheless, what we are talking about here is implementing good D&I practice across an organisation rather than enforcing a legal obligation on the workforce. It is this perception of enforced legislation that increases the risk of compartmentalisation and a tick-box approach. As such, it is this false perception of equality, diversity and inclusion that needs removing and this is where effective communication, workforce training and raising the profile of D&I can have a positive impact on its acceptance. Hence, improving the understanding of D&I becomes about the message and vision set out by senior leaders. Essentially, D&I is about people and it focuses on treating all people fairly and ensuring there is equality of opportunity across the workforce. Naturally, isn't this something we should all get on-board with? Unquestionably, fairness and equality of opportunity should be a priority for every organisation. As a result, the message needs to be very clear that D&I impacts on us all whether we be employees, employers, customers or other stakeholders including the communities we serve. For these reasons, we can see why good D&I practices must be embedded in all that we do.

Workplace Inequalities

Despite improvements to D&I practices in recent years we are still some way off seeing good practice embedded in all sectors. However, nationally, we are moving in the right direction and with continued support of organisations like the National Centre for Diversity, Stonewall, Athena SWAN, Diversity UK and the Employers Network for Equality and Inclusion, this should continue.

Roles such as EDI Coordinator, D&I Lead or Head of EDI have started to appear in the past five years across a range of employment sectors. Large employers are seeing the value in having strong D&I leadership in their organisations, especially in light of the poor press any high profile failures in D&I receive.

It's worth noting that despite lofty ambitions and employers hopes for inclusion in their own organisations, those with protected characteristics can still find themselves on the receiving end of bias, discrimination and prejudice in the workplace. As such, the need for organisational leaders to take ownership of D&I to combat inequality and unfairness in the workplace is still important. The following are just a few examples of workplace inequality, provided by the Trade Union Congress (TUC):

- **Black workers** have fewer training opportunities than white workers and black women get an even worse deal.

- **Older Workers** may have been in the job for longer but this may only mean that the longer you are in a job the less training you will receive.

- **Manual workers** and/or **workers with few qualifications** are mainly overlooked for training as those who have a lot of education and training tend to benefit from any training on offer.

- **Part-time workers** and **temporary workers** are often left behind when training is on offer as employers place a greater value on permanent or full-time workers at the cost of temporary or part-time workers. Women make up the majority of part-time workers.

- Workers for whom **English is a second language** may find that the only jobs open to them are manual / low skilled jobs. Whilst some will have qualifications, these may have been achieved in another country and employers will often overlook them. A lack of spoken English is often a barrier to moving on.

- **Shift workers** are least likely to participate in learning in colleges because of working patterns, or to be offered training by their employer. They may need to be encouraged when learning is promoted and shift times taken into account when onsite learning takes place.

- **Discrimination** often plays a role when access to job and training opportunities are based on negative stereotypes and perceptions of what people can and can't do.

Who Leads Diversity & Inclusion in an Organisation?

Hopefully you do. In a large organisation the leadership of equality and diversity may take a number of different forms ranging from the Head of Equality, Diversity and Inclusion to EDI Coordinator or Diversity & Inclusion Lead. Sometimes the role is a dedicated full or part-time role but other times it might be a secondary role of an existing manager. Frequently, with equality and diversity's focus being on people D&I leadership often falls to the Human Resources department.

Once in post, the D&I lead needs to establish what the expectations of role will be? Are there key performance indicators? How will performance or impact be measured? What does success look like? What is the vision for equality and diversity? However, it is also worth considering that one member of staff cannot singlehandedly change the culture of an organisation. Instead, the D&I lead needs to be able to form effective teams because only through collaboration and effective project management can success be achieved.
Furthermore, skills in influencing are vital because often the D&I lead will need to challenge and influence staff who he or she does not directly line manage, this is where high level skills in communication are essential.

When a clear set of goals have been agreed it is important to put together an effective action plan that can drive changes and the success of which is easy to measure. Targets set should be **SMART**, that is **S**pecific **M**easurable **A**chievable **R**ealistic **T**ime **B**ound. By using **SMART** targets, you have a better chance that they can be achieved because by being **Specific** you can focus on a small and specific action. Then, by making the target **Measurable** you know you can measure its completion or success. It may sound simple but by making the target **Achievable** you know that you are not asking for the impossible. When a target is **Realistic** it gives confidence to those who will be tasked with delivering the target that it can be done. Finally, when a target is **Time-bound** it gives you a clear time scale for completion and it is easy to measure whether something has (or has not) met its time scales.

The action plan below demonstrates the use of SMART targets to implement D&I actions in an organisation. RAG rating an impact column is a quick way to see where you are having the most impact and where additional support might be needed.

Issue	Action	Impact/Review (Date)
Job vacancy approvals are being issued with poor D&I consideration	All managers with recruitment responsibility to have D&I training by January regarding vacancy approvals to remove terminology such as 'join a young and dynamic company' or ' young person wanted'	Training undertaken, new vacancy approval forms show improvements to D&I good practice in 90% of cases

Asking Questions of your Organisations D&I Practices

The National Centre for Diversity[20] use the following exercise to help leaders take an informed view of how well D&I is led, managed and practiced within their own organisation.

Question	Y/N
My organisation has D&I policies that are in place.	
My organisation has D&I policies that are understood by all.	
My organisation has D&I policies that are followed by all.	
All of my colleagues feel that diversity is not just for minority groups, but includes everyone.	
Individual behaviours displayed by all staff are consistent with behaviours I would expect from an inclusive organisation.	
My organisation would look positively at adopting flexible working arrangements if these were requested.	
The behaviour of all of my colleagues makes me feel respected and valued.	
I know the difference between bullying and harassment.	
I have never witnessed inappropriate behaviour within my organisation.	
I have never witnessed bullying or harassment within my organisation.	
I feel that my organisation adequately invests in D&I.	
I feel that all of the managers and staff in my organisation are D&I confident.	
The building facilities and information materials are accessible to all people whatever their background or Protected Characteristic.	

Example Diversity and Inclusion Action Plan

By RAG (Red, Amber, Green) rating a review of the impact of D&I actions it can quickly be established where D&I actions are being met and where they need further attention. It is also a very useful way of demonstrating impact to senior leaders and letting them know where their intervention or additional support may be needed.

Issue	Action	Impact / Review
Lack of D&I steering group to challenge and lead D&I changes	Establish working group including board and Senior leadership and schedule monthly meetings **Who**: D&I Lead, HR director, representatives from front line, support and senior leadership **When**: 16.01.19	D&I Committee established and meets monthly with board and staff representation 1st meeting 09.01.19
D&I KPI's are out of date	Revise and Publish new D&I KPIs **Who**: D&I Lead **When**: 16.01.19	New D&I KPI's agreed at D&I committee meeting
Vacancy approvals are being issued with poor D&I consideration	All managers with recruitment responsibility to have D&I training regarding vacancy approvals **Who**: Managers with recruitment responsibility **When**: 14/01/19	New vacancy approval forms show improvements to D&I good practice in 90% of cases
E&D Action Planning awareness	E&D action plan to be shared with staff for consultation. Local action plans developed **Who**: All staff **When**: 28.02.19	E&D Action plan shared 16.01.19 Local actions plans requested for 28.02.19
Staff survey results are poor for question 8 – senior leaders embrace E&D	Senior leadership to undergo E&D training and discuss D&I in staff address **Who**: Board Members and Directors **When**: 28.02.19	Not yet achieved, training takes place 04.02.19

Implementing Diversity and Inclusion Good Practice

We need to empower our workforce to be able to effectively challenge D&I issues where they see them and drive transformative change in their own organisation. As such, Rohini Sharma Joshi[21], Trust Housing Association's EDI manager, asks that organisations consider the following four principals:

1. EDI is about people

We need to think about equality in a different way. [Your workforce] is fundamentally a people business and EDI is all about people - about treating them fairly and ensuring equality of opportunity, so these should be priorities for every organisation. We need to deliver a clear message that EDI affects us all as employees, employers, our customers and the communities we serve. That is why it must be embedded in all that we do.

2. Cultural change needs strong leadership

Embedding EDI in any organisation requires cultural change. It requires strong leadership and buy-in from the head of the organisation and senior management to take a meaningful step forward. There are several ways to amplify this message and to develop greater understanding of EDI issues including [organisational wide EDI strategic objectives, EDI charter or an initiative similar to] the Charted Institute of Housing's '10 by 20' challenge to meet 10 EDI objectives by 2020.

3. Engage with other organisations to share best practice

There are often valuable opportunities to learn from a variety of organisations within [any] sector, who also share a passion and commitment to achieving leadership excellence in EDI. At Trust Housing Association, we share our experience as part of our role as founding members of the National Centre for Diversity's new 'national patrons' network.

Trust was the first housing association in Scotland to achieve 'investors in diversity' status and, more recently, 'leaders in diversity' accreditation. This has enabled us to participate in a wider dialogue around issues that all kinds of organisations face in creating a diverse and inclusive working environment.

There are practical things the housing sector can do to address these issues. We have developed a training programme and we regularly discuss EDI issues in team meetings and with tenants, making it clear that discriminatory behaviour is not acceptable. We also publish case studies in our newsletters that underline the message that everyone is welcome and entitled to a safe and happy life.

4.   Make an action plan - not a wish list

A systematic approach to EDI does not show instant results but instead lays the foundations for change and develops well-informed and motivated staff who help build an inclusive organisation. If there is one thing [organisational] leaders must do to tackle EDI issues in [the next decade], it is to make sure that they are incorporated into a strategic action plan - not left languishing on a wish list.

Managing Change and Continuous Improvement

When implementing a change of practice (or culture) across an organisation (and many HR professionals will agree) there is the potential to be some workforce kick back to changes.

In an attempt to mitigate this kick back, as with any organisation wide change, the business case for a change to D&I practices needs to be shared with the workforce, to help get 'buy in' when implementing new processes. Better still, effective collaboration with the workforce prior to change is more likely to help with a transition to new practices.

In this way, the views of all staff can be consulted, collated and most importantly included so actions fed directly into operational action planning are representative of what the workforce perceive. This will help to ensure D&I actions are less compartmentalised and so not just the judgements of a single manager but a holistic, organisation wide, collective approach to implementing good D&I practice.

It's unlikely that D&I will be top of the agenda for managers across an organisation for various reasons. In most cases, it is because they have priorities of their own that need addressing and so D&I priorities fall down the list. When faced with a situation like this is important to support managers to embed D&I good practice rather than dictate that they must do it otherwise you risk it not happening and your leadership of the situation is easily called it to question. As such, work with managers and not against them, don't ask them to work harder… ask them to work smarter. However, the D&I leads own role in this is important because they need to examine the manager's priorities and demonstrate where D&I good practice can seamlessly fit into existing priorities and actions that are already planned.

As such, D&I goals can be met with little deflection from the area managers own priorities and hopefully with minimal conflict. It is only through collaboration, skills in influencing people and effective project management that D&I good practice can be embedded throughout an organisation. In most cases, embedding new D&I practices takes time and it is usually a subtle change but nonetheless significant in its impact.

It's important that we can measure changes and demonstrate the impact of our D&I actions. This is where statistics and other metrics are useful to show current progress on actions or indeed if an action is complete. For example, if you can report to senior leaders that the impact of D&I training has been a reduction by 33% of claims of harassment in the workplace then you are proving that it had a positive impact but that there is also some further work required to improve this figure still more.

The real secret to implementing change n an organisation, and there is a wealth of research on this topic, is to include the workforce in decision making. Where changes are a surprise and imposed on a workforce it's harder to get staff 'buy in' to the process, on the other hand where you have early consultation, collaboration and inclusion, research suggests, you will have better support to make changes from staff.

Equality Impact Assessments

An Equality Impact Assessment, often referred to as EqIA in the UK, is an internal audit process which is specifically designed to measure whether a policy, project or scheme is at risk of discriminating against any disadvantaged or vulnerable people. The EqIA remains a popular method throughout the UK as a means of checking internal polices, process and practices as organisations strive to ensure the public sector equality duty is being met in an organisation.

The purpose of the EqIA process is to prevent discrimination and where the assessment identifies a risk of discrimination action can be taken to make the necessary changes to ensure discrimination does not happen. In this way, the EqIA is a useful tool to help improve or promote equality in an organisation to help remove barriers and improve participation for underrepresented groups.

In most situations, organisations don't set out to purposefully discriminate against any of their stakeholders but sometimes a lack of awareness, especially where a policy, process or scheme may disadvantage one group over another, the EqIA can help to identify and make changes to ensure everyone is included and not disadvantaged.

Here is an example from ACAS, the Advisory, Conciliation and Arbitration Service, where they highlight how equality impact assessment can make a positive impact to the workforce. *'One local authority found a recipe for success over its meals on wheels service. The authority was concerned that the food it was serving up wasn't to everybody's taste. So it used an equality impact assessment to find out why. The authority discovered that in certain ethnic communities, only a few people were tucking in. So the authority decided to change the menu to ensure that these diners had a range of different types of meals more likely to appeal to choose from. Soon there were many more 'happy eaters' among these communities, while 'white British' users were also delighted at the improved choice and quality of the food. In this way the authority not only improved its service but saved money as well.'*

If a regular audit of an organisations policies, processes and practices is not undertaken then an unintended act of discrimination may remain undetected for some time, that is until someone makes a complaint or is let down by the service they receive. This is exactly how indirect discrimination happens in the workplace and an EqIA can be used to identify this early so changes can be made in the best interests of all.

Generally speaking, for an EqIA to be effective it must ask four key questions of what it is assessing. For example, if using an EqIA to assess the impact of a new policy then we must ask: 1.) What is the intention of the policy? 2.) How is it seeking to achieve this? 3.) Who benefits (and does not benefit) from the policy and how? 4.) What are any 'associated aims' (or other policies) attached to the policy and how do they impact? By doing this we can assess the intention of the policy, what method it uses to enforce the policy, who actually benefits from the policy and what other influences are there that impact on this policy, which should help us to identify risks.

Workplace D&I Training

It is likely when appointed as the D&I lead for an organisation there will be a training need in the workforce and a good D&I leader needs to be an effective staff development professional as well. As such, experience as a trainer or with staff development is valuable in a lead D&I role.

In general terms, D&I training can take two forms. Firstly, mandatory D&I training is usually some form of compulsory, self-directed, online, continuous professional development (CPD) of not more than an hour or two leading to level 2 certification in general equality and diversity awareness. There are many training companies that offer this on demand, low cost training on a licence basis so organisations can have their entire workforce trained, as and when needed.

Then there is the more specific training in the form of staff development where the business case for D&I good practice and other specifics can be addressed. Through staff development, organisation specific D&I training needs can be better addressed. For example, if a group of staff have been identified as having outdated views on women in the workplace then training on stereotyping and gender awareness can take place and we can look to re-educate staff with good D&I practice.

When providing D&I related training it is important to have a wide range of understanding in order to be able to provide training on the full spectrum of D&I related information, which may include:

- The Equality Act 2010
- Equality, Diversity and Inclusion
- Discrimination
- Disability discrimination
- Race discrimination
- Stereotyping
- Prejudice
- Values
- Beliefs and cultures
- Understanding sensory impairment
- Equality and human rights
- Bullying and harassment
- Children with medical conditions in school
- Age equality
- Communication

D&I training resources as well as text books on the subject are easily found on the internet to help support your training needs. However, it is important to take the time to know your subject well so that you can overcomes some of the barriers that will be presented in training as well as offering staff practical solutions to D&I related challenges. To this end, joining organisations such as the Institute of Equality and Diversity Practitioners (https://www.iedp.org.uk/) will help you stay up-to-date with the latest D&I news and training opportunities.

Make an Impact - Getting Things Done

Often, one of the most challenging aspects of leading diversity and inclusion in the workplace is actually getting things done, making an impact. It's easy to get lost in the rhetoric of equality and diversity, launching initiatives, giving training, explaining a vision… but in truth success is about what impact those things have. Have your actions made the workplace better for people? Have your actions reduced discrimination of underrepresented groups? Getting traction for your initiatives is vital so that you can measure the success of equality actions. However, one person cannot do this alone. In fact, there is a phrase often associated with parenting '*It takes a village*' which is true of equality and diversity as well. It takes the whole village, or in our case the whole organisation, to be supportive and actively involved in the D&I agenda to make it actually work, and by 'work' we mean make a positive impact on the work lives of staff with protected characteristics.

Fostering good, professional, working relationships are crucial when making changes to organisational culture and it is through these relationships that your D&I agenda can succeed. In a large organisation, you need to ensure that junior and middle management are supportive of your ambitions as it is these vital managers that will, ultimately, drive through your D&I actions. Support for your actions will not always be automatically forthcoming, especially where there are competing organisational priorities. However, this is where a good relationship and skills in negotiation and collaboration will serve you well.

Whatever priorities the manager decides are more important than your D&I priorities is not important because if you examine those priorities there will be opportunities to slip in D&I initiatives alongside. In this way, you are not asking managers to work harder, you are asking them to work smarter. In effect, you are supporting their goals and they are supporting yours, rather than competing against each other.

For example, if - as the D&I lead - you wanted to ensure D&I issues were included on meeting minuets across the organisation in order to capture a profile of D&I issues or to collate recorded concerns or success. You could make it a strategic action that all meeting agendas have an equality and diversity agenda item added as an organisational procedure. In that way, you can be sure that each and every meeting will have the option to highlight any equality and diversity issues, should they arise. In this way, you have only added a box to a standard agenda form, HR should be able to do this for you, which is not very demanding but in the same way you have not had to ask managers to forward you D&I concerns. All D&I issues highlighted in the meeting will be recorded in the meeting minutes, which in large organisations are usually saved online and can be easily shared with the D&I lead.

Where you do face a barrier to getting actions complete it is important to get strategic support from the senior leadership team. Where an D&I agenda is supported through an organisations strategic improvement plan it has a better chance of support from middle managers because it is a strategic priority for them as well. Ultimately, D&I initiatives need support form senior leadership, this support needs to be highly visible and those responsible for D&I need to work well with others.

The 1st 100 Days – Policy, Strategy & Quick Wins

An organisation needs to have a robust equality and diversity policy that sets out what the organisation will do to enforce the Equality Act 2010 and what it expects of its various stakeholders in regard to the Act. The policy should set out how bullying and harassment will be dealt with and how whistleblowing is managed. If your organisation does not have an equality, diversity and inclusion policy then it really should and you will need to create one. If you are unfamiliar with policy writing them work with your HR colleagues to develop one, examples can be found online as can examples from similar organisations who will likely publish them on their websites.

Policy - Where an D&I policy already exists, and it most likely will, then it needs reviewing to ensure it is up-to-date and fit for purpose. There is nothing wrong with a new set of eyes examining a document to ensure we are meeting our legal obligations. Reviewing your organisations D&I policy in the early days is an essential exercise, regardless of its need for changes or not. This is the document that you will be required to enforce across the organisation and through this policy you will be able make the organisational changes where you encounter them.

Strategy - An effective strategy to support your D&I agenda is vital. Sometimes, D&I actions are included in an organisational strategic improvement plan. Certainly, for an D&I agenda to be successful it will require strategic support and vision from senior leaders. However, if you are going to be adding strategic objectives for equality and diversity then it is also important that you know what needs to be improved.

As such, early in your role as D&I lead your will need to establish what your D&I priorities are going to be for the year ahead and this is where you could refer to the self-evaluation questions in the section - *Asking Questions of your Organisations D&I Practices* – earlier in this book. When you have a clear idea of what needs to be improved then you can implement informed and SMART actions or objectives for the strategic plan.

Quick Wins - There are a number of quick wins and easy to implement good practice procedures that can help put you on the road to an inclusive culture more rapidly, these can include:

- Introduce/promote a Flexible Working Policy, including working from home;
- Establish D&I Steering Group to drive D&I agenda across the organisation;
- Display key D&I messages on organisations displays, screen savers and other communications systems, such as Microsoft Yammer;
- Include an D&I prompt/section on 1 to 1 forms for meetings between managers and staff to ensure D&I issues are discussed regularly;
- Introduce gender neutral toilets & a quiet room for prayer and devotion;
- Get the boss involved and ask leaders to publically promote D&I values;
- Offer mental health and wellbeing training to all staff;
- Through annual appraisal ensure all staff undertake mandatory online D&I training as CPD.

Reporting Impact of D&I Measures to Leaders

Senior leaders and governance must be regularly informed as to the progress of diversity and inclusion improvement measures so initiatives can be better supported where they are not being embedded effectively. Success stories are always nice to be able to report to senior leaders but where barriers exist to equality and diversity implementation managers can argue the case for senior leader support to remove these barriers.

Often, D&I data is reported in terms of percentages, such as 83% of staff have completed mandatory, online D&I training. However, percentages only tell us part of the story and what is needed is evidence based opinion of the impact of that 83% having completed the training. For example, if you can say that 83% of staff have completed mandatory D&I training and the impact of this has been a reduction of 50% in staff complaints of discrimination… then we are reporting more effectively on the benefits that, in this example, staff training has had on the workforce.

Progress can be demonstrated in a number of ways, including through recognition with national regulatory bodies such as the

National Centre for Diversity. Their Investors in Diversity scheme is a benchmark for organisations to demonstrate commitment to inclusion in the workplace. If you can achieve an award, such as Investors in Diversity, then your organisation will have demonstrated that it has met a national standard and is an inclusive workplace for staff, which will go some way to demonstrate that you are meeting your own D&I strategic targets.

Organisations like the National Centre for Diversity as well as Stonewall, Disability Confident or Inclusive Employers can help you demonstrate your organisations commitment to inclusion through partnership programmes.

In truth, when reporting to senior leaders, an ongoing action plan with current progress on actions and targets will provide sufficient information regarding the success of your D&I agenda. On the other hand, when reporting to governors or a governing body a more formal, annual report approach may be necessary. Indeed, changes to language may be necessarily as the governing body or board members may not be specialists and adapting your communications methods to suit your audience may be necessary.

When considering what to report it is important to consider the phrase 'so what?' as it will focus your efforts on the impact of actions rather than the completion of actions. For example, similarly to the previous example using percentages, if 80% of middle managers have completed a training session on discrimination you could ask... 'so what?' In effect, we are asking what has the impact been of middle managers undertaking this training, and again much like the example earlier, we can capture the impact of this by stating, for example, that this training has led to a 35% drop in part time workers claiming discrimination for a lack of training opportunities.

Ultimately, when reporting to senior leaders a summary of the progress D&I initiatives have made is what they need and this can be kept relatively brief. Specifically, they will want to know...what has happened, what was the impact and what barriers are you facing in completing the D&I agenda?

National Centre for Diversity, Stonewall & Inclusive Employers

There are a number of groups that can help organisations to develop inclusive cultures through diversity programmes, but there is a cost involved for their service.

Below are links to the National Centre for Diversity, Stonewall and inclusive Employers who all run a partnership programme to help build workplace diversity and inclusion. Also, there is Disability Confident from the UK Government which helps customers and other businesses identify those employers who are committed to equality in the workplace.

Web Site Address	Programme
https://www.nationalcentrefordiversity.com	Investors in Diversity
https://www.stonewall.org.uk	Stonewall DIVERSITY CHAMPIONS
https://www.inclusiveemployers.co.uk/	National Inclusion Standard Gold
https://disabilityconfident.campaign.gov.uk/	disability confident EMPLOYER

Part 3 – Workplace Strategies to Improve Diversity & Inclusion

Hints, Tips & Other Strategies to Build Inclusion

Over a decade ago, the Chartered Institute of Personnel and Development[22] undertook research into recruitment and retention in the workplace. They concluded that employers who employed people from a range of different backgrounds, of different ages and those who bring different life experiences to the workplace could make an organisation more competitive and help solve problems in recruitment. What is surprising is not the outcome of this research but that it was over a decade ago and the UK workplace can still suffer from poor inclusion and diversity.

To that end, when trying to build diversity in the work place it is important to think outside of the regular recruitment box, widen your influence and be seen by different and underrepresented groups as a welcoming employer who respects the differences in its employees and the benefits that can bring to the organisation. To this end, below are a range of strategies that will help bring about inclusion in your organisation.

- Workplace commitment to diversity in induction training material for new staff;
- Recognise religious festivities in workplace agreements;

- Provide a quiet room for prayer and devotion;
- Demonstrate a commitment to equality in sexual orientation by actively promoting that benefits available to the spouses and dependents of your employees also apply to gay partners;
- Be age friendly, make sure bias has not crept into your recruitment and promotion policies. Check phrases in job adverts don't discriminate on the basis of age, such as 'become part of a young, dynamic team' or 'young person needed';
- Widen where you advertise your organisation – you might be missing out on a pool of talent by only using familiar recruitment methods, for example advertise in an ethnic minority newspaper or sponsor events to different groups;
- Hold a series of workshops for staff on particular D&I topics;
- Use workplace intranets and other internal methods of communication to share D&I information and best practice;
- Publicise workplace diversity related achievements, such as being awarded Investors in Diversity or becoming a Stonewall Champion;
- Provide and publicise access to training and development opportunities to all;
- Introduce programmes to help improve skills in written and verbal English;
- Provide a single point of contact for people with a disability who can provide support and specialist equipment;
- Provide flexible work options including home based and job sharing;
- Use staff surveys or a diversity audit to identify areas of weakness;
- Ensure all job descriptions included a demonstrated commitment to workplace diversity;
- Provide access to a free, confidential Employee Assistance Programme.

Advancing Equality for Disabled Staff

Workplace equality and diversity initiatives have grown in recent years and have focused on a range of protected characteristics identified in the Equality Act 2010. However, much of that focus has been on Race, Sexual Orientation, Gender Reassignment and Religion. Yet, disability affects almost one if five of the UK population and statistically disabled people are more likely to be unemployed or economically inactive.

Primarily, the Equality Act 2010 should focus our work on advancing equality of opportunity between people who share a protected characteristic and people who do not share it as well as fostering good relations between people who share a protected characteristic and people who do not share it.

The Disabled Living Foundation[23] explain that disability is still often misunderstood, especially in the case of mental health, and getting a better understanding of the lived experiences of our disabled staff must be a priority for employers. Only by having this understanding and input from staff can we actually advance equality of opportunity for disabled staff in the work place. Furthermore, by raising awareness of disability issues we can encourage organisational wide discussion and foster good relations between people with a disability and those without.

Some facts about disabilities in the UK:

- There are around 13.3 million disabled people in the UK (almost one in five of the population).
- 5 million disabled people are in employment, compared to 2.9 million in 2013.
- In January 2016, the UK employment rate among working age disabled people was 46.5% (4.1 million), compared to 84% of non-disabled people.
- Disabled adults are nearly three times as likely as non-disabled adults to have no formal qualifications, 30% and 11% respectively.
- The average income of families with disabled children is £15,270, which is 23.5% below the UK mean income of £19,968. 21.8% have incomes that are less than 50% the UK mean.

Getting a snapshot of disabled staffs workplace experience

Large organisations need a snapshot of the experiences of their disabled staff in key areas. By providing comparative data between disabled and non-disabled staff, this information can be used to understand where key differences lie; and will provide the basis for the development of action plans, enabling organisations to track progress on a year by year basis. This provides a mirror for the organisation to hold up to itself, to see whether or not it sees a reflection of the communities that it serves.

Ramadan Mubarak – How to Support Employees Observing Ramadan

In 2019, Ramadan began on Sunday 5th May and ended on 4th June in the UK, and those observing the holy month will be fasting and taking part in religious practices for 30 days.

Working Muslims will be fasting from sunrise to sunset every day, which could be around 17 hours of not eating or drinking every day for 30 days.

Neil Payne[24], writing for HR Zone, explains although fasting is usually the primary association with Ramadan, the month involves a lot more exertion than refraining from food and water. Eating your first meal at sunset, extra prayers, late nights and a heightened emphasis on patience and virtue are all part of experiencing the holy month.

Best practice for Ramadan at work

- Establish when Ramadan is approaching and who this could affect at work. Muslims will not mind if asked about the upcoming month and without having to be direct, one should be able to know whether or not they will be fasting.
- Ensure all staff that work with Muslim colleagues are aware of what fasting entails and how this could impact someone. Fasting 17 hours a day is not easy and colleagues need to appreciate how this can translate into behaviour and working practices.
- If shift work is the norm, look at any changes that can be made to offer those fasting the opportunity to swap shifts or change their working hours in a way that suits all parties.
- For those in 9-5 roles, consider flexitime options for start and finish times. See if allowances can be made for people to work lunch hours and breaks in return for an earlier finish.
- Asking a Muslim to attend a lunch meeting demands a lot of them. Many may politely agree, as will many decline. Be understanding of those that do not feel comfortable sitting and watching people eat and drink.
- If welcoming someone into your office for a meeting who you believe could be fasting, simply ask on arrival if they want a drink. If they decline you can be pretty sure they are fasting and there is no need for you to keep offering them a tea and biscuits.

- If you bring food and drink out onto the office floor, do not allow it to be placed right next to the desk of someone fasting. If you normally eat your lunch at your desk, try and show some discretion. However, the vast majority of Muslims won't mind as its part and parcel of Ramadan in the UK.
- Make special allowances for Muslims to take a break at sunset to break their fast if they happen to still be on shift. This needs to be ample time to break their fast, pray and then eat properly.
- If you have a canteen, try and arrange for some meals to be saved for people fasting so they are not left choice less at the end of their day.
- Avoid booking in meetings for the afternoon. If high concentration levels are needed from people, don't expect this after lunchtime. Use the morning when people are still relatively fresh.
- Do not expect people to commit to evening functions. The evenings are dedicated to eating, prayers and gatherings within the family and wider community.
- You may find some staff booking of up to 2 weeks towards the end of Ramadan. There is a practice whereby men spend the last 10 days living in the mosque to help intensify their acts of worship. Be accommodating in allowing this period off ensuring it does not clash with company guidelines.
- Be prepared for people to take between 1-5 days holiday at the end of Ramadan to celebrate Eid. This has the emotional equivalent to Christmas and is the one time of the year whole families and neighbourhoods get together to share presents and good food.
- If fasting team members are working remotely, work out time differences and how their daily routine will impact you in terms of meetings, deadlines, SLAs, etc.
- Try and use Ramadan as a platform for greater understanding and improving team dynamics. Why not throw an iftar one evening and allow people to share a part of their lives with colleagues?

Flexible Working for New Dads

The role of the working mum is well-established; however in recent years we have seen the rise of the working dad. Increasingly, dads are making more requests for flexible working arrangements than ever before. In fact, a recent study by daddilife.com[25], produced in association with Deloitte, found that nearly two thirds (63%) of dads have requested a change in working pattern since becoming a father.

According to the study, modern day fathers are more involved in parenting than ever before. In fact, the study claims 87% of the dads surveyed are either mostly or fully involved in day to day parenting duties. So much so that dads are increasingly putting fatherhood ahead of their careers, or at least accepting the need for a better balance between work and home life after the birth of a child.

Requests for flexible working patterns might include asking to spend a day or two working from home every week. Perhaps so they're present for the nursery run, or for half an hour of play and interaction at lunchtime. Likewise, the need for flexible working could be for compressed or reduced hours, so new dads can spend more time with their children during those crucial early years. Whatever it is, new dads are asking for more flexible working in record numbers. This is because, more than ever, they value time spent with their young families.

The study suggests that millennial dads are prepared to take drastic action to make sure they achieve a lifestyle that is good for work and good for their families. The research found that a third of dads had already changed jobs since becoming a father. In addition to that a further third were actively looking to change jobs. That's an interesting finding as far as employers are concerned. It shows that offering flexible working for parents (both mums and dads) is likely to help them retain their top talent.

The study also suggests that, at the moment, too many organisations are letting good workers drift into the arms of other organisations. Specifically, the ones who are more sympathetic to the need for better flexibility at work.

The worry is that not all employers are getting the message. For instance, the Deloitte research reveals that, while 14% of dads have requested to work from home on one or two days a week, less than one in five (19%) have had the request granted. Similarly, 40% of the dads interviewed have requested a change in working hours but nearly half of them (44%) have been turned down.

Dads are increasingly reporting that the greatest life satisfaction comes from being an involved and present parent. Too often though, they bump up against a workplace environment that is sadly out of touch with that sentiment.

Nearly half (45%) of working fathers regularly experience tension from their employer when trying to balance work and family life, while 37% regularly experience tension from colleagues, and 45% with their partners.

Society may be gradually more accepting of the fundamental role that fathers play in creating happy, well-adjusted children, but many workplaces are lagging behind. As a result, dads are suffering because of that, and organisations are too. Unhappy workers are never at their most productive.

Improving LBGT Inclusion in the Workplace

I have recently been working with Stonewall[26], the leading lesbian, gay, bisexual and transgender rights charity in the United Kingdom, when an organisation I worked for partnered with their Diversity Champions Programme.

People perform better when they can be themselves, and we should all be looking to make sure that lesbian, gay, bi and trans (LGBT) staff are fully included in the workplace and Stonewall have some useful tips to help.

1. **Ensure that your policies are fully inclusive of LGBT people**

This includes pensions, family and leave policies, health insurance and relocation allowances. You should make sure your policies explicitly mention LGBT people.

2. **Get people involved across your organisation**

This could include setting up a network group specifically for LGBT employees; they'll help you know where you're doing well and which areas may need a new approach.

3. **Reward those involved in your LGBT network group**

Embed their involvement in their appraisals; make being part of the network a desirable thing to be.

4. **Decide upon a clear strategy and tactics**

Whether you want to increase the number of staff who are open about being LGBT, or revise your policies to make them fully inclusive, it's crucial to know where you want to be and how you're going to get there.

5. **Engage staff members who don't identify as LGBT**

Allies, as we call them, are a crucial element of ensuring inclusion for all. They can help spread the message that diversity is celebrated by your organisation.

6. Ensure senior support

Making certain your senior leaders actively communicate their support for LGBT inclusion sends a positive message of acceptance for all across your organisation.

7. Speak to your staff

Consulting employees – both LGBT and non-LGBT – about what inclusion looks like in your organisation will help ensure your strategy is appropriate and that all staff share your vision.

8. Understand your staff

Getting to know the make-up of your staff through techniques such as monitoring will help ensure you effectively cater to any needs they may have.

9. Celebrate your successes

Making sure your organisation is LGBT-inclusive is an ongoing journey, so it's important to celebrate your successes, whatever size they may be, along the way. Every step is a step towards acceptance without exception for LGBT people.

10. Become a Stonewall Diversity Champion

Diversity Champions is Britain's leading programme for ensuring that your workplace is fully inclusive and more information can be found at https://www.stonewall.org.uk.

Positive Action for Under Representation

Positive action is very often a misunderstood or misrepresented term. Unfortunately, some still talk of it as a deliberate act by Human Resources to recruit more ethnic minority staff into an organisation. Its misunderstandings such as this that show positive action must not be confused with positive discrimination, which is illegal.

Positive action is where you identify that your workforce is under represented in a specific area and do something about it. For example, as we have seen in recent years, many UK Company boards are under represented by women and companies have taken positive action to address this. Positive action in this case could be to promote board vacancies specifically to woman in the organisation, or to have a leadership programme for board members of the future that actively encourages participation by woman. However, you will notice that the example above does not dictate that UK Companies hire only woman and discriminate against male applicants to solve the issue - which would be illegal - it simply asks that we make the effort to involve woman, promote our board vacancies to woman and encourage them to apply. Though, it's worth noting, despite much work to improve the representation of women on the boards of UK Company's it has done little to increase representation of women of colour in these roles. As such, further work is still needed in this area for boards and governing bodies to be truly representative of the community we serve.

As such, positive action can be defined as the voluntary actions an employer takes to address an imbalance of opportunity or disadvantage that an individual with a protected characteristic could face in the workforce. Positive action can be used wherever your workforce is under represented or is not reflective of the community it serves including (but not limited to) age, disability, ethnic minority, LBGT+ or gender.

A good example of where positive action can look to redress an imbalance is in construction industry where there are only 3 female apprentices for every 98 male apprentices. As such, positive action here might be to better promote the construction industry to girls in schools and other educational settings, or to show progressive imagery on construction industry posters and advertisements which show woman in construction roles.

I often hear senior leaders actively supporting the business case for diversity in the workplace but I don't always see an effective strategy of positive action to meet the business case. Diversity is the celebration of the differences between us and valuing the how those differences make our workforce stronger. Diverse experiences can lead to diverse solutions in the workplace. If you hire the same type of people all the time you will get the same outcome all of the time. As such, ensuring your business has diversity in its workforce can ensure that you have diverse solutions amongst your staff.

The first challenge then is to know where your workforce lacks diversity. The only way to do that is to examine the make-up of your own staff and ask yourself the following question: does your workforce represent the community it serves? But this is a big picture situation. We need to examine the context of the community you serve. For example, if you generally serve a region of the UK then you need to look at the make-up of that region. If the latest Government Census indicates that the population of that region predominately - say 95% - identify as being ethnically white British then how does your workforce compare? Again, you can look at gender and establish what percentage of the community is female and what percentage are male and compare that to the make-up of your own workforce. The same applies to those members of the community who identify as disabled or LGBT+. Only when you know the make-up of the local community can you identify what aspects of diversity you actually need to improve.

Subsequently, only when armed with this knowledge can you then look to positive action to help recruitment build you a more diverse workforce.

Staff Networks

Staff networks can be a powerful tool for empowering minority groups to have an effective voice in an organisation. In the context of diversity and inclusion, a minority group is a group of individuals who are known to have been discriminated against on the basis of a shared characteristic. It is worth noting that these groups may not be a minority in terms of numbers as in the case of women, who are a minority group, despite comprising over half of the UK population.

According to Advance H.E.[26] (formally the Equality Challenge Unit), staff networks may not work in every workplace and/or for all minority groups, and their viability and success will depend on the culture and demand within individual organisations.

Networks need to be led by the staff groups that they represent. However, there is a role for institutions to facilitate and support the development of networks:

- Involve staff and discuss the need for staff networks. This could be linked to specific times of year to maximise impact, for example discussing the possibility of a women's network on international women's day. A specific event gives the opportunity to discuss whether it is viable and to look for volunteers to take the network forward.
- Provide a budget. From refreshment for meetings, to organising specific events or training and development, a budget of any size helps to ensure the network is sustainable and effective.
- Ensure senior management are open to dialogue. Networks can provide a useful perspective on institutional practice. Consultation should be genuine and views of the network taken seriously.
- Publicise networks to all staff. A dedicated area on your website/intranet means that all staff are aware of support and opportunities. Promote the networks during staff inductions to maximise membership and ensure all staff are able to benefit.
- Create a culture of acceptance for participation. It can be intimidating to join a network and there can be a perception that members of networks are 'troublemakers'. Ensure line

managers encourage staff to attend meetings in work hours. Senior management engagement can help to legitimise the group, and positive endorsement can underline that taking part is worthwhile.

Aims and Objectives

1. Sharing experiences and providing advice and support in a confidential safe space

Often a staff network is the opportunity staff members have to discuss the challenges they have faced at work. To meet this aim, it is likely that membership will be limited to people with the particular shared characteristic. Organisations need to carefully consider how, when and where the group will meet, and how to get a balance between giving an opportunity to share personal experiences while retaining momentum and developing positive solutions.

2. Working collectively towards improving institutional policies and practices and implementing change

Networks with this aim can be useful for their members and their institution. They can raise concerns from members, act as a consultation group for policies and practice and help to generate ideas and solutions.

However, to be successful and to maintain momentum, the organisation has to listen to the network and genuinely involve them in decision making and policy review.

Terms of Reference

Networks can have a variety of terms of reference, depending on their aims and context. These may also develop over time as the group evolves. The language used in describing and naming networks can also be crucial in their success and who joins.

Know the Diversity & Inclusion Calendar

Annually, there is a wide range of recurring D&I events dedicated to supporting equality, diversity and inclusion across the globe, some last a month others just the day. Whilst individual dates do vary for the events listed below, year on year, they generally fall within the months shown. By celebrating an event in the workplace it can be the catalyst for specific conversations and highlight the challenges other communities face.

- **January** - Holocaust Memorial Day, World Braille Day, World Religion Day and World Braille Day
- **February** - LGBT History Month, International Day of Women and Girls in Science and Chinese New Year
- **March** - International Women's Day, International Day for the Elimination of Racial Discrimination
- **April** - World Autism Awareness Day, World Health Day, St George's Day and Stephen Lawrence Day
- **May** - World Day for Cultural Diversity for Dialogue and Development, International Day Against Homophobia, Ramadan and International Day of Families
- **June** - Gypsy, Roma, Traveller History Month, World Refugee Day, Eid-al-Fitr
- **July** - Gay Pride Events, Nelson Mandela International Day
- **August** - International Youth Day, International Day for the Remembrance of the Slave Trade and its Abolition, World Humanitarian Day, International Day of the World's Indigenous Peoples
- **September** - World Suicide Prevention Day, International Day of Democracy, World Contraception Day
- **October** - Black History Month, UK Older People's Day, World Mental Health Day and National Hate Crime Week
- **November** - Armistice Day, Transgender Day of Remembrance, International Day for Tolerance
- **December** - International Day for Persons with Disabilities, Rosa Parks Day, Human Rights Day

Part 4 – Case Studies – Inequality in Action

Case Study 1 – Community Tensions

The Equality and Human Rights Commission provides the following case study[28] highlighting how Fenland District Council worked to preventing community tensions and tackling stereotypes.

Fenland District Council has one of the largest Gypsy and Traveller populations in the East of England. The Council currently manages five permanent Traveller sites on behalf of Cambridgeshire County Council. It has developed a site with both space for permanent residents and temporary travellers. Individual family plots, as well as a large number of private sites are also available. This is successfully run on its behalf by an agent with Traveller heritage who is also helping people within the community develop their skills.

Action taken

The Council has been proactive in engaging with Gypsy and Traveller communities. It has built up a good relationship with them and provides advice on making planning applications, advice on land acquisition and the development of privately-owned sites. It also develops skills within the community.

Benefits

Provision of the sites has laid a good foundation for community relations in the area. The on-going engagement means that Travellers contact the Council when they want to set up a site, rather than taking the unauthorised route. Good site provision has also meant that Gypsy and Traveller issues are no longer attracting negative press coverage. The Portfolio holder for Gypsy Traveller issues at Fenland District Council, stated: "by providing good sites we avoid many of the problems associated with Gypsies and Travellers, which gave them a bad name and attract bad publicity."

Finally, the provision of sites has enabled Traveller children to grow up aware of their Gypsy heritage while having access to basic services such as schools and hospitals.

Case Study 2 – Racial Discrimination

When the English Football League kicked off in August 2019 the opening weekend was marred with a number of incidents of racist abuse. Like any other employer in the UK, a professional football club has a duty under the Equality Act 2010 to protect its staff from racial abuse. The Equality Act makes no distinction as to the type of workplace, a football player is a member of staff and the football pitch is a workplace.

On Saturday 3rd August 2019, Southend United's Jamaican striker Theo Robinson – Speaking to the BBC[29] - claims he was abused "in front of family, friends and their kids" at St Andrew's, the first match Coventry have played in their ground-sharing arrangement with Birmingham City. Similarly, Stoke City's James McClean, Barnsley's Bambo Diaby and the sister of Fulham's Cyrus Christie were also victims of what's been described as "unacceptable discriminatory abuse".

Anti-racism charity Kick It Out said "On the first weekend of the season, these incidents should be a reminder for everyone in football that racism and discrimination cannot be ignored. Clubs and the football authorities must be relentless in calling out this disgraceful behaviour, and be prepared to issue strong sanctions and education sessions to any supporter involved. Discrimination casts a shadow over football in this country, and we will not stop highlighting the problem while it remains rife in the game."

Whilst in this case the racial abuse is coming from a minority of fans in reality a football fan is a customer of the club and a consumer of the clubs product or service. As such, this is no different from hospital staff receiving racial abuse from a patient or service user. In such cases, NHS Trusts work to support staff and reduce racial abuse happening and football clubs must do the same. However, we hear much more outrage from the public and political leaders when NHS staff are racially abused. Why then are footballers, as well as other sports men and woman, seen as fair game to abuse at work?

Certainly, the money involved in football infuriates many fans, especially when they are being charged £40 a ticket and another £50 for a replica club shirt. They see the elite football players earning the big bucks and see themselves as effectively their employers. Oddly, if they were the employers then by law they should treat their staff better. That said, we know that when a football team is doing well the fans sign their praises from the stands but when things are not going well a minority of fans abuse the players, regardless of ethnic origin. This abuse from the stands has almost become a 'norm' but race is a protected characteristic under the Equality Act and harassment on the basis of it is illegal, just as would the abuse of a disabled member of staff, or an LGBT+ member of staff. In fact, I am sure the ongoing situation with racial abuse of players is contributing to the lack of any visible LGBT+ professional football players. Unfortunately, LGBT+ players are not confident enough in being accepted by all fans that they have to hide that aspect of their lives away and as such lead an unauthentic version of themselves, in itself this can lead to anxiety, depression and other mental health issues.

So what are clubs to do? In reality, expulsion from the ground and permanent exclusion from all football grounds is a strong deterrent. Clubs must demonstrate their commitment to stamping out racial abuse but those fans that do not racially abuse players must also be given the confidence to challenge the abusers and show them that this behaviour is not okay.

Either way, the Equality Act 2010 protects all staff from abuse in the workplace and unless clubs do more to protect their players from racial abuse they could be in breach of the Equality Act and subject to legal action.

Case Study 3 – Gender Discrimination

The Writers' Guild of Great Britain recently commissioned a report which suggests the number of female writers working for film and television in the UK has not improved in the last 10 years.

Lucy Todd$_{30}$, Entertainment reporter from the BBC, highlights the shocking statistic that only one in 10 feature films is written chiefly by a woman, the figure dropping even lower for those with a budget greater than £10m - to just one in 14.

The Guild is calling for change in the industry and having worked in post 16 education I can see the problems start when students are young. Better information and guidance as well as aspiring female role models are needed in the classroom in order to inspire the next generation of female writers. However, attitudes in film and television studios need to change, diversity needs to be respected and sort out whilst opportunities must be for all, regardless of gender or any other barrier to success.

Hollywood has been under fire for a number of years regarding its gender equality and hit the headlines recently when Patty Jenkins, director of feature film 'Wonder Woman', called out the industry on its record of female directors. In the UK, Fleabag, Happy Valley and Ordeal By Innocence are among the few TV shows to be written by women.

Writer and presenter Sandi Toksvig is also among those to give her support to the campaign, saying: "There is no shortage of talented women writers in the UK, and therefore no excuse that so few of them are getting commissions in film and TV."

Screenwriter Kay Mellor said: "It's criminal that I can count on one hand how many women signature writers there are on TV right now. Sometimes it takes a collective to say - 'this is not fair' and it's not. It's time things changed."

Case Study 4 – Under Represented Groups

The government is published its review of higher education tuition fees and post-18 funding in the 2018. Coupled with the recent introduction of the Office for Students to hold the sector to account, Universities in England are facing significant change.

As a result of these changes, widening participation has become one of the primary focuses of the newly established Office for Students. Subsequently, Higher Education providers who want to charge the maximum course fee of £9,250 per year will be expected to have an access and participation strategy designed to support the recruitment of students from under represented groups.

Part-time study has traditionally supported under represented groups by allowing, those whose outside commitments restrict their ability to undertake Higher Education full-time, an avenue to study at this level. However, significantly, part-time study also offers an opportunity for higher education to those returning to education after a period out of full time education. In my experience, part-time study is often taken up by those returning to learning after an absence from full time education and it's this return to study where adults can retrain or gain new industry skills to further employment opportunities.

The Confederation of British Industry (CBI) says university should not only be for young people, and adults need to be able to re-train for new skills. However, as Sean Coughlan[31], BBC News education and family correspondent, highlights in the article below, there is a worrying trend in our University sector where part-time student numbers are 'down by more than half' since 2010.

The CBI and Universities UK have requested more support for students to take short, flexible part-time courses and they warn of a generation of "lost learners" who might previously have gone back to study for part-time degrees or other qualifications. Subsequently, in light of the governments drive to improve the employability of graduates - where Destination of Learners in Higher Education (DLHE) data will be measured by the Office for Students - it is a worrying trend and Universities must adapt in order to be responsive to the needs of part-time students.

82

That said, the report highlights the significant "rise in tuition fees" which has been a particular deterrent for part-time students, who might have jobs and family responsibilities and were reluctant to take on such levels of debt. So, the question has to be, what can Universities in England do to provide a higher education service to part-time students that is short, flexible and provides either academic or industrial updating. Ultimately, before any decisions are made its important to establish what part-time learners actually want from studying in higher education. Are they studying for personal interest reasons or are they trying to upskill themselves for employability purposes? That said, having seen a 50% decline of part-time learners in eight years it begs the question... what have Universities done differently in the past eight years that has contributed to this decline? If the rise in tuition fees is a contributing factor then what support can be put in place to make part-time fees more affordable with flexible payment options to spread the cost in a similar way to full-time learners.

In the BBC article, Matthew Fell, the CBI's policy director, said: "Too often we think of universities as being just for young people, but as this work shows, adult education and lifelong learning matter just as much."

"Universities need to play a critical role in responding to the changing world of work by offering education and training for learners for whom a three-year bachelor's degree doesn't quite fit their circumstances," he said.

Case Study 5 - Exclusion

Councils across England are obliged to make every effort to reduce their NEET (Not in Education Employment or Training) numbers which identify how many young people in the region are not actively involved in education, employment or training. In the main, Councils will work closely with schools to identify pupils who are at risk of not being involved in education, employment or training when they leave school whilst supporting the schools intervention strategies. Worryingly, where schoolchildren are excluded from education there is a significant rise in their likely hood to become NEET.

However, a recent report by Barnardo's[32] highlights a worrying trend that excluded schoolchildren are at serious risk of becoming involved in knife crime, the children's charity has warned. Barnardo's says excluded children are also at risk of "being groomed and exploited by criminal gangs".

The charity said 47 councils, about one in three in England, had no spaces in pupil referral units (PRU), which look after excluded children. The government said a review of school exclusions and their impact on children was ongoing.

The research, which was carried out in collaboration with the All Party Parliamentary Group on Knife Crime, shows a 56% rise in exclusions in England since 2014. The group's chairwoman, Sarah Jones, said knife crime was at its highest level on record and "our schools are on the front line". She added: "Exclusions are rising and in many cases there is literally nowhere for those children to go. This is heart-breaking." She said excluded children were "marked as failures", and added professionals often talk about the "PRU to prison pipeline".

Barnardo's chief executive, Javed Khan, said: "We know children excluded from mainstream schools are at serious risk of being groomed and exploited by criminal gangs." He urged the government to reduce the number of pupils excluded from schools and to improve alternative provisions so "vulnerable young people get the help they need to achieve of positive future".

A government spokesperson said: "Permanently excluding a child from mainstream school should only ever be a last resort, and we support teachers in making these difficult decisions where they are justified." They added the government was undergoing a review of exclusions led by the former education minister Edward Timpson.

The spokesperson said: "We are transforming alternative provision to improve outcomes for these children which helps them to flourish, backed by our £4m innovation fund that has created nine new projects around the country."

Summary – Culture first, Diversity & Inclusion Second

If there is one key message that you take from reading this book, then I hope it is that diversity and inclusion is not just about compliance with legislation, it is about leading change, implementing improvement initiatives and engaging, motivating and improving the potential of staff.

Sundar Pichai, chief executive officer of Google LLC, said of inclusion "A diverse mix of voices leads to better discussions, decisions, and outcomes for everyone."

This is equally true of the boardroom as it is the operational side of an organisation and the distinction that equality is not just about compliance with legislation must be supported at board and executive level within an organisation in order for diversity and inclusion initiatives to have any real impact.

As such, the first job to improve diversity and inclusion in an organisation is to get board and executive backing. Furthermore, unless the culture of the organisation is right then no diversity programme will help. Accordingly, before any diversity and inclusion initiatives are rolled out it is essential that the culture of the organisation is one which is receptive to change, to new ideas and inclusion.

Where an organisations culture does not yet lend itself to inclusive practices then wholesale organisational development is essential and any diversity initiatives will fail until that culture is fixed. Organisational design and re-structuring is the subject of a number of books for human resources leaders and beyond the scope of this book.

Where you have a workplace culture which supports change and new ways of working as well as the visible support of the board or executive leadership then you have a solid base for building diversity and inclusion in the organisation.

Good diversity and inclusion practice recognises that historically certain groups of people with protected characteristics such as race, disability, sex and sexual orientation have experienced discrimination. To that end, an organisations equality strategy must be about ensuring that every individual has an equal opportunity to make the most of their working lives and talents.

Furthermore, a good diversity and inclusion programme or strategy attempts to ensure that no one should have poorer life chances because of their gender, their race, the way they were born, where they come from, what they believe, who they love, or whether they have a disability.

As a final point, in order to improve diversity and inclusion in the workplace, it is absolutely vital that we don't just think about the data; we need to collaborate with people because the organisations people – whether that be staff, customers or service users - are at the heart of all successful diversity and inclusion improvements. Only through working with their people can an organisation reduce bias in hiring, foster inclusivity and create feelings of belonging for employees of all backgrounds.

"A lot of different flowers make a bouquet."

Muslim Origin

Diversity & Inclusion – A Glossary of Terms

Below is a brief explanation from Jan Lawrence at In-Equilibrium[33] of the main terms used when discussing Diversity & Inclusion:

- **Equality** - Fair treatment of individuals or groups, ensuring they are treated equally and no less favourably in areas including those of age, disability, gender, race, religion or belief, sexual orientation, gender re assignment, marriage and civil partnership, pregnancy and maternity.

- **Direct Discrimination** - Treating a person less favourably than another is being treated, or would be treated, because of their protected characteristic(s). Direct discrimination also includes:

- **Associative Discrimination** – when an individual is discriminated against because of their connection with someone who has a protected characteristic(s).

- **Perceptive Discrimination** – being discriminated against because it is believed an individual possesses a protected characteristic(s). It applies regardless of whether the individual possesses the protected characteristic(s) or not.

- **Diversity** - Acknowledging, valuing and respecting people's psychological, physical and social differences in order that their full potential and contribution can be realised.

- **Inclusion** - A sense or feeling that an individual or group are welcome, respected, supported and valued in order that their unique needs, working and learning styles are met. An inclusive environment will embrace differences and offer respect both verbally and in actions to ensure that everyone can fully participate.

- **Indirect Discrimination** - Happens when an organisation's conditions, policies or practices which, on the face of it appear neutral, have an impact that particularly disadvantages those who share a protected characteristic(s); unless whoever applied it can provide 'objective justification.'

- **Harassment** - The Equality Act 2010 defines harassment as, "unwanted conduct related to a relevant protected characteristic, which has the purpose or effect of violating an individual's dignity or creating an intimidating, hostile, degrading, humiliating or offensive environment for that individual." Harassment applies to all the protected characteristics except, Marriage and Civil Partnership and Pregnancy and Maternity. Employees can complain of behaviour that they find offensive even if it is not directed at them and they do not possess the relevant protected characteristic themselves.

- **Positive Action** - Is distinct from unlawful positive discrimination (which involves the practice of favouring an individual who belongs to a group which suffer discrimination). Positive action is lawful when an employer takes steps to counteract the disadvantages it believes people who shared a protected characteristic face. Any decisions taken following positive action must then be made on merit (unless section 159 of the Equality Act 2010 applies).

- **Protected Characteristics** - The Equality Act 2010 specifies 9 features which, for the advancement of equality and opportunity, are afforded protection from discrimination, harassment, and victimisation. In alphabetical order they are: Age, Disability, Gender, Gender Reassignment, Marriage and Civil Partnership, Pregnancy and Maternity, Race, Religion or Belief, Sexual Orientation.

- **Reasonable Adjustments** - The duty to make reasonable adjustments is covered in the Equality Act 2010 to ensure positive steps are taken to remove the barriers those with disabilities face so they are not substantially disadvantaged.

The 3 main areas organisations and establishments need to consider are:

- To change provisions, criterions or practices which may provide a barrier unless it is unreasonable to do so

- To change a physical feature of a business or premises which may make access or use difficult for those with disabilities

- To provide auxiliary aids or services, which may include additional services, in order to help a person with a disability to either access or do something

- **Stereotype** - A widely held, positive or negative, image or idea which an individual believes about the characteristics of a certain group.

- **Victimisation** - Occurs when an individual is singled out for unfair treatment or discrimination as a result of making a complaint/grievance, threatening to make a complaint/grievance or supporting a complaint/grievance made by a third party.

References

1. Vijay Eswaran, World Economic Forum, The business case for diversity in the workplace is now overwhelming, https://www.weforum.org/agenda/2019/04/business-case-for-diversity-in-the-workplace, 09/19
2. Union Learn from the TUC, Equality and diversity – what's the difference?, https://www.unionlearn.org.uk/equality-and-diversity-whats-difference, 02/2019
3. Frances O'Grady, Breaking Through The Barriers, Unionlearn, 2012
4. Leading Series 2013, Managing Equality & Diversity, BBP Learning Media, 2013
5. Jiten Patel and Gamiel Yafai, Demystifying Diversity, Gilgamesh Publishing, 2016
6. Nerlarine Cornelius et al., Building Workplace Equality, Thompson, 2002
7. University of Sheffield, Equality Act, Protected Characteristics, https://www.sheffield.ac.uk/hr/equality/focus/2.5491/protected, 02/2019
8. Citizens Advice, Discrimination, https://www.citizensadvice.org.uk/law-and-courts/discrimination/, 02/19
9. Government Equalities Office and Equality and Human Rights Commission, Equality Act 2010: guidance, https://www.gov.uk/guidance/equality-act-2010-guidance, 02/19
10. Robert Booth and Aamna Mohdin, Revealed: the stark evidence of everyday racial bias in Britain, The Guardian, https://www.theguardian.com/uk-news/2018/dec/02/revealed-the-stark-evidence-of-everyday-racial-bias-in-britain, 02/2019
11. ACAS, Bullying and harassment , https://www.acas.org.uk/bullying, 02/19
12. Equality and Human Rights Commission (EHRC), What is the European Convention on Human Rights?, https://www.equalityhumanrights.com/en/what-european-convention-human-rights, 02/19

13. ACAS, Public Sector Equality Duty,
    https://www.acas.org.uk/index.aspx?articleid=5990, 09/19
14. Pamela Duncan, Niamh McIntyre and Caroline Davies,
    Gender pay gap figures show eight in 10 UK firms pay men
    more than women, The Guardian,
    https://www.theguardian.com/world/2019/apr/04/gender-
    pay-gap-figures-show-eight-in-10-uk-firms-pay-men-more-
    than-women, 02/19
15. Aleksandra Wisniewska, Billy Ehrenberg-Shannon, Cale
    Tilford and Caroline Nevitt, Gender Pay Gap: women still
    short-changed in the UK, Financial Times,
    https://ig.ft.com/gender-pay-gap-UK-2019/, 09/19
16. Lora Jones, BBC News, What is the gender pay gap?
    https://www.bbc.co.uk/news/business-42918951 09/19
17. The Fawcett Society, What is the gender pay gap?,
    https://www.fawcettsociety.org.uk/close-gender-pay-gap,
    09/19
18. Equality and Human Rights Commission (EHRC), Gender
    pay gap reporting enforcement plan
    revealedhttps://www.equalityhumanrights.com/en/our-
    work/news/gender-pay-gap-reporting-enforcement-plan-
    revealed 09/19
19. Dharshini David, BBC News, Gender pay gap: Five things
    to bear in mind, https://www.bbc.co.uk/news/business-
    47824183, 09/19
20. National Centre for Diversity, 5 Min Health Check,
    https://www.nationalcentrefordiversity.com/home/quiz/,
    02/19
21. Rohini Sharma Joshi, The Chartered Institute of Housing,
    Equality, diversity and inclusion: four top tips,
    http://www.cih.org/news-
    article/display/vpathDCR/templatedata/cih/news-
    article/data/Equality_diversity_and_inclusion_four_top_tips,
    02/19
22. The Chartered Institute of Personnel and Development,
    Recruitment and retention in the workplace
    https://www.educationandemployers.org/wp-
    content/uploads/2014/06/recruitment-retention-and-
    turnover-cipd.pdf, 02/19

23. Disabled Living Foundation, Key Facts, https://www.dlf.org.uk/content/key-facts, 02/19

24. Neil Payne, HR Zone, Ramadan at work: HR best practice, https://www.hrzone.com/perform/people/ramadan-at-work-hr-best-practice, 09/19

25. Hugh Wilson, Daddie Life, The Millennial Dad at Work, https://www.daddilife.com/the-millennial-dad-at-work/, 09/19

26. George Alabaster, Stonewall, Top 10 tips for LGBT inclusion in the workplace, https://www.stonewall.org.uk/node/41639, 09/19

27. Advance HE, Staff Networks, https://www.ecu.ac.uk/guidance-resources/employment-and-careers/development-progression/staff-networks/, 09/19

28. EHRC, 2009. 'Gypsies and Travellers: Simple solutions for living together' and Fenland District Council, 02/19

29. BBC Sport, Kick It Out 'appalled' after four incidents of racist abuse at weekend, https://www.bbc.co.uk/sport/football/49236509, 09/19

30. Lucy Todd, BBC News, Call for action on UK's screenwriter gender inequality, https://www.bbc.co.uk/news/entertainment-arts-44209815, 09/19

31. Sean Coughlan, BBC News, Part-time students 'down by more than half' https://www.bbc.co.uk/news/education-45979230, 02/19

32. BBC News, School exclusions 'fuelling gang violence' - Barnardo's, https://www.bbc.co.uk/news/uk-46027265, 02/19

33. Jan Lawrence, in-equilibrium, Equality & Diversity – A Glossary of Terms, https://www.in-equilibrium.co.uk/equality-diversity-glossary-terms, 10/19

34. John Duncan et al., Various articles, https://www.theequalityblog.co.uk, 10/19

Notes:

_____

_____

_____

_____

_____

_____

_____

_____

_____

Notes:

Notes:

_____

_____

_____

_____

_____

_____

_____

_____

_____

Printed in Great Britain
by Amazon